Guitar Wizard

Walije Gondwe

© Copyright Walije Gondwe 1991

All rights reserved. No reproduction, copy or transmission of this publication may be made without written permission.

No paragraph of this publication may be reproduced, copied or transmitted save with written permission or in accordance with the provisions of the Copyright, Designs and Patents Act 1988, or under the terms of any licence permitting limited copying issued by the Copyright Licensing Agency, 33-4 Alfred Place, London, WC1E 7DP.

Any person who does any unauthorised act in relation to this publication may be liable to criminal prosecution and civil claims for damages.

First published 1991

Published by MACMILLAN EDUCATION LTD
London and Basingstoke
Associated companies and representatives in Accra, Auckland, Delhi, Dublin, Gaborone, Hamburg, Harare, Hong Kong, Kuala Lumpur, Lagos, Manzini, Melbourne, Mexico City, Nairobi, New York, Singapore, Tokyo.

ISBN 0-333-54227-4

Printed in Hong Kong

A CIP catalogue record for this book is available from the British Library.

Illustrations by Gary Rees

Chapter
1

"Mrs Onyango, I think Wezi's going to be a pop star."

"Why do you say that?" asked Mrs Onyango, very surprised.

"Well, because he likes music so much," answered Mrs Sweeny.

"Do you think so?"

"Of course. Haven't you seen him listening to the radio?"

"We haven't got a radio," Mrs Onyango said. "His father took it away when he left us."

"Just watch this then."

Mrs Sweeny picked up a little red radio and found some pop music. Wezi immediately bounced up and down and waved his hands with the music. As he did so, a big smile came over his face.

"You see what I mean?" Mrs Sweeny was almost as excited as Wezi. "Look at him. He loves it. And he's not even a year old yet."

Wezi's mother had to agree.

"You're right," she said. "I never knew it before. I've been so worried about money and finding a job and everything else. I just didn't see it."

"You should get him a radio," laughed Mrs Sweeny, shaking the radio in her friend's face. "You could be looking at a pop star here."

"A pop star! I hope not," said Mrs Onyango seriously. What a foolish idea!

"Why? What's wrong with being a pop star?"

Sometimes Mrs Onyango couldn't understand English people. How could they be serious about the world of pop music like this? She had been brought up in Malawi, and in her family people did not become pop stars. They worked hard and had good, safe jobs, like doctors or teachers.

She tried to explain.

"Well, in England it may be all right, but not in Africa," she said. "We shall go back there one day. Wezi's got to go to school here and pass his exams first. Then he'll be able to get a good job in Malawi."

"A pop star's not a bad job. Look at all the money they earn," Mrs Sweeny pointed out.

"I know, but it's not a real job, is it? I know this is London, and the Swinging Sixties and all that, but a pop star! It's . . . it's . . ."

Mrs Onyango gave up. She would never make her friend understand. Education was so important in Africa. It was what all the mothers wanted for their children. And she was going to do her very best for her son, even though she was on her own now.

Wezi was still bouncing up and down, loving the music that poured out of the little radio.

"This is 1969, not 1869! It's London!" Mrs Sweeny said. "These days young people choose their own jobs. They want to enjoy their work. That's the most important thing for them."

Mrs Onyango didn't believe a word of it. And to be a pop star! Well that was not for her family!

Mrs Sweeny was still watching Wezi.

"Just look at him. He's got music in his blood, Mrs Onyango."

"Please call me Tumeki," Wezi's mother said with a smile. In England people often called each other by their first names. If she was going to stay in England for a while, she felt she should try to follow some of the English ways.

"Thank you, Tumeki. There really is something special about Wezi, you know."

"I can see it now. You're right, I shall have to buy a radio."

As Tumeki said this a worried frown crossed Mrs Sweeny's face. Tumeki's life was difficult, and her friend knew it. Wezi's father had left, and Tumeki was a long way from her own country and her own family. She had two children, Wezi and his sister Biku, to bring up all alone in London.

"Can you afford a radio?" Mrs Sweeny asked. "I don't

want to be rude, but..."

"It's all right," Tumeki laughed. She knew why the other woman was worried. "I haven't told you my good news yet. I've got a job. I start work on Monday. And as soon as I've saved some money, I'm going to get a radio for Wezi."

"Tumeki, I'm so glad. That's wonderful."

Tumeki's face was all smiles.

"Everything's going to be OK. I've got a job and somewhere to live. Things really are getting better."

"What about Wezi and Biku?" Mrs Sweeny asked. She had often looked after Wezi while Tumeki looked for work. She really loved the little boy. "What will you do with them?"

"Biku already goes to school, so she's no problem. Wezi's got a place at Woodchurch Day Nursery. I shall take him there in the morning on my way to work, and collect him afterwards."

"Are you sure? He's very young."

"It's the best thing for him. The teachers are all very good. *And* they have lots of music. He can sing and dance all day long."

Mrs Sweeny laughed.

"He'll have music at school and the radio at home. What more could he want?"

Wezi laughed too. But that was because the music on the radio was very loud and very fast. Just what the little boy liked best.

Chapter 2

Wezi started at Woodchurch Day Nursery soon afterwards. Tumeki was very glad that Wezi could go there. He would be safe while she was at work.

Wezi was not so glad. At first he didn't like the nursery at all. He cried and screamed when Tumeki left him there.

"Poor Wezi," said Mrs Crosby, the lady who ran the nursery. "You want to go with Mummy, don't you? Never mind. You'll soon get used to us."

She showed Wezi some toys. Soon he stopped crying and started to play with them.

Outside the nursery, in the garden, there was plenty of space. The older children could run around and play, and there were lots of things to do. Inside there were toys and games and the children could look at books and paint pictures or even watch television.

As the months passed Wezi loved Woodchurch Day Nursery more and more. He didn't cry when Tumeki left him there in the morning. He cried when she took him home instead!

The best thing of all was the music.

When the record player was on, Wezi knew all the songs. When Mrs Crosby brought out the drum, he banged the hardest. When the children sang, his voice was the loudest. When the children danced, his feet moved the fastest.

Mrs Crosby knew how much Wezi loved music, and on his third birthday she had a good idea. She bought a surprise present for him.

"Happy birthday, Wezi," she said, giving him a parcel. "Here's a present for you. Don't open it here. Wait till you get home."

The parcel was wrapped in pretty blue paper, and Wezi couldn't wait to open it.

He put his parcel on the table. Tumeki wanted to help him, but Wezi said,

"No, Mummy. I'll do it. I'll open it."

He always wanted to do things himself, even if they were really too difficult.

He tore the blue paper off the parcel.

"Look, Mummy. Look!"

The present was an Elvis Presley suit, just like the real Elvis wore.

"Let me put it on, let me wear it now," Wezi shouted. He was very excited.

"It's lovely," Tumeki said. "Isn't Mrs Crosby nice?"

Wezi ran into the bedroom and took off his clothes as fast as he could. He wouldn't let Tumeki help, even though the buttons were difficult. Then he put on the Elvis Presley suit.

He looked at himself in the mirror for a long time, left to right and up and down.

The jacket and trousers were white, but they had silver buttons and a silver pattern all over. Wezi had seen a picture of Elvis wearing the same suit. He thought it was wonderful.

"Look, Mummy. I look just like Elvis," he cried.

Tumeki agreed.

"You look really good," she laughed.

She laughed even more a few minutes later.

Wezi looked at himself for a long time. Then, still in front of the mirror, he started to sing one of Elvis's songs. At first he sang quietly to himself, but the sound got louder and louder until soon he was singing at the top of his voice. And as he sang he started to dance. First he tapped one foot on the floor, then the other. Next he turned from side to side. After that he lifted his arms, and clapped and waved and soon his whole body was moving, shaking and rocking.

He looked just like Elvis Presley! What's more, he sounded like him too. Wezi liked being a pop star very much indeed.

At the time Tumeki thought it was funny. If only she had known!

Wezi liked his suit so much that he wanted to sleep in it that night. His mother had to say,

"Elvis doesn't sleep in his clothes."

Then Wezi agreed to take the suit off. But it had to be in bed with him.

The next morning Wezi put the suit on again. He wanted to show it to all the other children at the day nursery. After that he wanted to wear it every day. Sometimes his mother had to hide it.

As Wezi grew bigger and bigger, the Elvis Presley suit got tighter and tighter. He still wore it every day, but the trousers became tighter than Elvis's.

On his fourth birthday Tumeki bought him a toy guitar. Wezi couldn't play it, but he didn't care. He put on the suit, picked up the guitar, and sang and danced all day long, just like the famous American pop star.

Chapter 3

When Wezi was five years old he went to a primary school near his home in London. He liked it from the very first day, as most young children do. He was a very friendly child, and popular with everyone. In those days there were only five black children in the school. But to Wezi and everyone at the school people were people and friends were friends. Colour made no difference.

He was quick to learn and Tumeki was pleased to see how much he enjoyed his lessons. Most of all, however, Wezi loved the lessons where he could sing, and maybe dance or clap in time to music.

When he was about seven years old Wezi wanted to have piano lessons at school. The lessons were very expensive, and his mother had to pay for them. This wasn't easy for Tumeki, because she still didn't have a lot of money.

"How much do piano lessons cost?" she asked the teacher.

At first, when the teacher told her, Tumeki shook her head. Then she thought again. If the other children were learning to play the piano, Wezi was going to learn too. She was determined to do her best for her son.

"All right," she said at last. "I don't have to pay school fees for you here in England. And the piano is a very nice hobby for you."

Tumeki was right and wrong. She was right because playing the piano was very nice. She was wrong because it was not just a hobby for Wezi. Neither of them knew it then, but music would become the most important thing in Wezi's life.

All that was a long way ahead for Wezi though. At the time he just enjoyed his piano lessons. He was very quick to learn a new tune. So he was a little surprised when his teacher gave him a large book one day.

"What's that for?" he asked. "I want to play the piano, not read books."

"The music you've just played is written down in this book. You have to learn to read music, just like you learn to read words," his teacher explained.

Wezi thought that this was a waste of time. Already he could hear a tune on the radio and play it with one finger on the piano. He could even make up new tunes in his head and play them.

"If you can write down your music in a book you'll never forget it," his teacher pointed out. "And what's more, other people will be able to read it too."

Wezi could understand that, so he learned to read music as well as play it. But he still liked playing best of all.

Wezi had real talent, and the piano teacher soon saw it. He told Wezi to practise every day. This was a problem because Wezi didn't have a piano at home. The piano teacher told the headmistress, who said,

"Wezi, you can stay in the classroom after school and practise every afternoon."

Usually Wezi did this, but sometimes he was tired and just went home. This didn't happen very often because Wezi loved his music.

It worried Tumeki though. She didn't get home from work until six o'clock, and Biku, Wezi's sister, had to look after him until then. But Biku had her own friends and wanted to play with them.

"Why do I have to wait for Wezi?" she complained. "I never know when he's coming home. I can't do anything I want to do. It's not fair."

Once Biku even went out, and Wezi had to sit outside the house until Tumeki got home. It was all very difficult.

Then Tumeki thought of an answer to the problem. She and Wezi went to see the piano teacher together.

"Do you think Wezi could practise on a cheap children's organ?" she asked.

"Well it's better than nothing," the teacher said. "Wezi has real talent."

Tumeki was very proud when she heard this.

Wezi was saying,

"Please, please, please, please, *please* let me have my own organ." But he was saying it to himself, not out loud.

His mother must have heard the message though, because the next day Wezi and Tumeki went out together.

They went to a real music shop. It sold pianos and organs, guitars and drums, and musical instruments that Wezi had never seen before. It was the first time that Wezi had been in a music shop. He thought he was in heaven!

He tried every organ in the shop, even the most expensive ones. He touched; he listened; he played. He had a wonderful time.

It took hours, but at last Wezi chose an organ. A man brought it to his house the next day, and after that Wezi practised every single day.

With the lessons at school, and the little organ at home to practise on, Wezi learned to play the piano really well.

Chapter
| 4 |

Just before Wezi started secondary school he and Tumeki went away for a holiday. They stayed in an expensive hotel by the sea. It had taken Tumeki a long time to save the money for the holiday.

But at first she didn't enjoy herself very much.

The weather was good, and there were lots of interesting things to see and do. Tumeki and Wezi went out every day.

The hotel was nice too. They had a big, comfortable room, and the food was fine. After all those years in London Tumeki was well used to English food.

No, the problem was that Tumeki was lonely.

She and Wezi were the only black people in the hotel. So she felt they were different from the other guests. And although there were plenty of guests, none of them talked to her. They weren't rude, or nasty, or anything like that. They just didn't speak to her.

English people aren't like Africans. They aren't so friendly, they won't chat to strangers, they don't get to know each other quickly.

Tumeki understood this, and usually it didn't worry her. In fact she felt sorry for the English. Life didn't seem to be much fun for them.

But soon something happened which made their holiday much more fun. Something which shows that people of any country can be shy themselves, and are ready to greet you and be friendly once they feel they know a little about you.

There was a piano in the hotel, and Wezi could play it whenever he wanted to.

There was a big organ too. Sometimes a man came and played for the guests at night, and Wezi and Tumeki always went to listen to him.

When the man was playing Wezi couldn't just sit still and listen. He tapped his feet and clapped his hands and sang the tunes to himself. All very quietly, of course.

But at last he couldn't keep quiet any longer.

"Mum, can I have a go on the organ?" he whispered to Tumeki.

"Don't ask me. Ask the man."

"Shall I?" Wezi said, smiling with excitement.

Wezi got up and walked straight over to the man at the organ. He was having a break, enjoying a glass of beer and smoking a cigarette. He put his glass down on top of the organ and smiled warmly at Wezi.

"Hello, young man. What's your name then?"

"Wezi."

"What?"

"Wezi. W-e-z-i."

"Oh, Wezi. I don't think I've heard that name before. What does it mean?"

"It means 'blessing'."

"That's lovely. And what can I do for you, Wezi?"

"Please can I have a go on your organ?"

"Of course you can. Come on, let's see what you can do." The man picked up his glass and moved to another chair.

Wezi sat at the organ. He waited for just a few seconds, and then he began to play.

He was brilliant!

He played old songs and new songs, fast tunes and slow tunes, music that people knew and music that they had never heard before.

All the guests stared at him, then at one another, then at Wezi again. When he stopped playing they clapped and cheered and shouted,

"More, more. Play some more."

The man at the organ got to his feet. He was also clapping and smiling.

"Ladies and gentlemen, give this young man a big clap," he said. "He'll soon put me out of a job."

Everybody laughed and cheered even more.

The hotel visitors smiled at Tumeki too, and she nodded her head at them. One woman came and sat next to her, then another, and then a third. They all thought that Wezi was wonderful.

Tumeki was very proud of her son.

"You were very good," she said to him when at last he returned to his seat.

Wezi loved it. He was not at all shy about playing in front of all those people. He loved having an audience. In fact he enjoyed it so much that when the hotel owners asked him to play the next night, he almost ran to the organ.

Tumeki did not try to stop him. She knew it would be a waste of time. But she was surprised that her son had so much talent.

After that Tumeki wasn't lonely any more. She and Wezi made lots of friends in the hotel.

The cheap organ had done a good job after all.

Chapter 5

Playing the organ in the hotel changed Wezi. Before this he liked to play for himself. Now he liked to play for other people too. Music became more and more important to him.

As soon as he got back from his holiday he went to the music stores in Denmark Street, in the centre of London. There he saw something fantastic.

He tried to explain it to Tumeki.

"It's called a synthesiser. It's the latest thing. It looks a bit like a piano, but it can sound like any instrument you choose."

"What do you mean?"

Wezi tried again.

"Listen, Mum. It's not difficult to understand. It looks a bit like a piano. If I want it to, it can sound like a piano. But if I want it to, it can also sound like a guitar or an organ or any other instrument."

He showed her a picture.

"That's a piano," Tumeki said, looking at the picture.

"No, Mum, it's not a piano. It's a synthesiser. It looks like a piano, but it can sound like a guitar or anything else. It can do so many different things that music will never be the same again."

Wezi took his mother to the shop in Denmark Street to see the synthesiser. Tumeki could hardly say the word, never mind understand it.

She sat in a corner of the shop while Wezi tried the synthesisers. He went from one to another enjoying every moment. She was very surprised. One minute Wezi played and the synthesiser sounded like a piano. The next minute the same synthesiser sounded like a guitar!

The owner of the store showed Wezi how to play and explained all the technical details. All very serious!

When the man was too far away to hear, Wezi whispered, "He thinks you're going to buy one for me."

Tumeki was cross with Wezi.

"I haven't got the money for that."

"OK, Mum. I know. But if you weren't here he'd never let me play with the synthesisers. And I just had to have a go."

That was typical of Wezi. If he really wanted to do something, nothing would stop him.

Wezi didn't get a synthesiser. He did get a guitar though. It happened like this.

When Wezi was twelve his sister Biku bought a guitar. She wanted to learn to play it. Perhaps she dreamed of being a pop star herself. The walls of her bedroom were certainly covered with pictures of different groups. She was a real fan.

Unfortunately Biku and the guitar did not get on very well. She passed it down to Wezi, and went back to things that she did well, like painting and cooking.

Unlike his sister, who needed a good guitarist (like a pop star!) to teach her, Wezi taught himself to play the guitar. He was glad that he could read music now. His piano teacher had been right.

Soon he was spending most of his pocket money on books of guitar music, and on guitar strings, which kept breaking. He said it was normal for guitar strings to break! It was also *very* expensive!

Now he spent hours every evening in his bedroom.

"Wezi, time for food," his mother would call.

"In a minute," would come the answer.

Ten minutes later.

"Wezi, your food's cold."

"In a minute." The same old answer.

Wezi had discovered something exciting. The pop songs on Tumeki's old record player sounded even better when he played his guitar at the same time. And the louder the sound, the better he liked it.

Chapter
| 6 |

Wezi made a new friend in school at this time. The friend's name was David, and – you've guessed right – he loved music too.

David had an electric guitar. The two boys spent hours playing together and listening to records and tapes.

Wezi and David started to go to gigs. As you know, when a singer or a group plays in a club or a hall somewhere, and people buy tickets to go and listen, that's a gig.

They usually enjoyed themselves. Loud music, bright lights, hundreds of teenagers all packed together into a hall – fantastic.

Once, however, Wezi and David had a bad time. It wasn't at a gig itself, though Tumeki was always telling them to look out for trouble.

No, the bad time happened when they were on their way to a gig. Wezi and David were walking past the Royal Free Hospital when two policemen stopped them. One policeman took Wezi across the road, and the other one stayed with David.

Wezi didn't understand what was happening. Tumeki had always told him that the police were there to help. So why were these two being so horrible?

"Where are you going?"
"What's your name?"
"Where do you live?"
"What are you doing here?"
"Why are you walking past the hospital?"

The questions came thick and fast. Both Wezi and David answered each one, telling the truth every time. At last the policeman questioning Wezi took him back to David.

"I think they're OK," he said. "Let them go."

Wezi wanted to know why they had been stopped and

why the policemen had asked all those questions. He was upset, but he still wanted to know what was going on.

"What's the matter?" he asked. "Why did you stop us?"

"There are lots of thieves around the hospital," one of the policemen answered. "They're stealing from cars. We're looking out for them."

"But we've never stolen anything," said Wezi. "Why did you think it was us?"

The policeman seemed surprised.

"Youngsters like you. You must have been stopped before."

"Well *I* haven't," Wezi answered. "Have you, Dave?"

David shook his head.

The policemen let the two boys go. Later on, when Wezi told Tumeki, she was very, very angry.

"Why did they stop *you*, Wezi? I'm sure it's because you're black. They wouldn't have stopped David by himself, would they? I'm going to ring the police station this minute and complain."

Tumeki went over to the telephone.

"No, Mum. Don't do that," Wezi said, calmly.

"Most of the blacks in this country are good people. They work hard and they just want to live their own lives. But the police often treat them like criminals. It's not fair."

"It doesn't matter, Mum. Really, it doesn't worry me."

"Well it worries me," Tumeki burst out. "The police are supposed to treat everybody the same, black or white. This is racism, nothing else. They should be ashamed of themselves."

"Mum, it happens all the time and not just in this country. I've got to learn to deal with it myself."

Wezi was wise for his age, but his mother was still far too angry to listen.

"The police make problems for themselves," she went on. "If that's the way they treat black people in London, I'm not surprised they have trouble."

"That policeman didn't even realise that he was being racist," said Wezi. "That makes it worse. But I've got to live with it. They'll learn in the end."

"What about David? How did he feel about it?"

"He got very upset, especially when he thought about it afterwards," said Wezi. "But we agree. We can't argue with the police at our age. It's best to stay out of their way."

"Do you agree about most things?" asked Tumeki. "Even though you're black and David's white?"

Wezi looked at his mother seriously. He shook his head in surprise.

"Of course. We think the same way. We're on the same wavelength. Thinking the same way as other people has nothing to do with the colour of *their* skin or yours. My friends *are* my friends because we like doing and talking about the same things. That's all there is to it."

Tumeki saw there was a lot of truth in this. But in the end she wrote a letter to the chief of police. She told him that the police were sometimes wrong. She told him that some policemen were racists, even if they didn't know it. She told him that this made the lives of black people very difficult and unhappy.

Tumeki hoped that the chief of police would read the letter and that things would get better.

Chapter
7

When Wezi was fourteen he and Tumeki went to Malawi for a holiday. It was the first time that he had ever been there, so he was very excited.

Tumeki had often talked about her own country, and her family there, so Wezi thought he knew a lot about Africa. But he had no idea what it was really like.

The surprises started the minute the aeroplane landed at the airport. Wezi thought the English summer was hot. Now he knew what hot weather meant. He thought he would melt!

And the family! Wezi knew that he had aunts and uncles and cousins, but they all seemed to be at the airport. Who were all these people? One after another they threw their arms round him and kissed him.

The biggest surprise of all was Tumeki. She had wanted so much to go "home". She had talked so much about her family. She had looked forward to Malawi even more than Wezi had. But now that she was really there, she was crying!

Wezi couldn't understand his mother at all.

Through all this Wezi hung on to his guitar. He had been determined to bring it to Malawi, and he didn't want to lose it now.

He was swept into the back of a car with his cousins. His Uncle Kanyerere sat in the front with Tumeki. They had a long drive to Uncle Kanyerere's house.

Wezi couldn't believe he was really in Malawi at last. Everything was so exciting. The colours were so bright. The sounds were so clear. The smells were so fresh. And everybody was smiling.

Wezi got used to Malawi after a few days. He met all his aunts and uncles. His cousins took him around the town where they lived. Everybody knew about him, and greeted him. He felt that he really belonged there. He loved it.

He was so busy at first that he had no time to play his guitar. That didn't last for long, of course. Wezi couldn't live without his music.

One night he took his guitar outside and played quietly to himself. After a while Uncle Kanyerere heard him and came out to listen.

Uncle Kanyerere was an engineer; he had a very good job. Tumeki wanted Wezi to be just like Uncle Kanyerere when he grew up. She wanted him to do well at school and pass exams and study so that he would have a good job too.

Tumeki had quite forgotten that Uncle Kanyerere loved music. When he was at school he was famous for his musical talent, just like Wezi. He played the guitar and sang and danced brilliantly. If Uncle Kanyerere had had his way he would have been a star. He understood how Wezi felt about music.

Uncle Kanyerere listened to Wezi for a long time. Then he said,

"Wezi, that was wonderful. You make me feel young again."

Uncle Kanyerere sat quietly for a few more minutes. He was thinking, remembering the old days, while Wezi played quietly on. At last he said to Wezi,

"You love music, don't you, my son?"

"I do," answered Wezi.

"I was like you when I was young," said Uncle Kanyerere. "I had your talent. But I never made the most of it."

"Why was that?" Wezi asked. He didn't want to be rude, but he really wanted to know.

"Oh, lots of things happened. The family didn't have much money, and my father worked hard to send me to school. I had to study at university. Then I had to get a good job, earn some money to help my brothers and sisters. It wasn't a good idea for me to be a musician."

"Do you mind, Uncle?"

Uncle Kanyerere thought for a long time before he answered.

"I made the right decision," he said at last. "I have a good life. I can look after my own family, and I enjoy my work as an engineer. It was the right decision for me, but what's right for me may not be right for you. You have to live your own life, Wezi."

"I know," said Wezi, very seriously.

Uncle Kanyerere stood up.

"That's enough talk for one night," he said. "Tomorrow you're going to listen to your own music. Music from Malawi. I've heard you play Western music, and now it's time you heard something else. You're African after all, and our music's part of you."

After that Uncle Kanyerere took Wezi to hear African musicians. Suddenly it seemed that everybody in Malawi played or sang or danced.

Wezi saw and heard things that he had never dreamed of, and he loved it all. The music here was alive. It was fresh, different, exciting. And it was everywhere.

Wezi was very interested in all the different instruments. Some of them he had never seen before, but he tried them all.

He was most interested in the kalimba. A kalimba is a thumb piano, and it makes a lovely sound. A very old man, a friend of Uncle Kanyerere, taught Wezi how to play it. It was quite difficult, but Wezi didn't give up.

At the end of the holiday, just before Wezi and Tumeki went back to England, there was a festival in the town. There was singing and dancing, and music, of course. The atmosphere was wonderful, and everybody was very excited.

Wezi was the most excited of all. For one thing he had never been to a festival. But even better than that, he was going to play the kalimba.

He didn't play alone. In Malawi people always played in groups, with lots of different instruments. And he didn't play for long, just while Uncle Kanyerere's friend rested. But he did play.

It was fantastic. The music wasn't written down, the musicians didn't need that. Somehow everybody just knew when to play and how to play, and everything came together. Wezi made his own music and managed to fit in with the other musicians. Wezi couldn't explain it, but it was brilliant.

Wezi had never enjoyed himself so much. It was the best day of his life. He knew that even when he was back in England the kalimba and the music from Malawi would stay a part of him.

Chapter
| 8 |

Back in London Biku's old guitar wasn't good enough for Wezi any more. But neither was there enough of Wezi's pocket money to buy an electric guitar.

"Mother, I've saved some money in the bank," he said. "Can I use it to buy an electric guitar?"

"You certainly cannot," answered Tumeki. "That money's for your education. I won't let you waste it on something stupid like a guitar."

Wezi had a real problem, but as usual he found the answer himself.

One Saturday afternoon he left the house with his guitar. He didn't tell his mother where he was going. He didn't tell her a lie, but he didn't tell her the truth either.

Tumeki thought that Wezi was going to David's house. What he actually did was walk to Hampstead station.

There he bought a ticket to South Kensington, and got on the underground – one of the trains that run under central London, in other words.

South Kensington is a very rich part of London. People there have plenty of money. Some of the biggest stores are there too, and at the weekend it's always very busy.

Wezi didn't even leave the underground station at South Kensington. Instead he found a good place at the top of some stairs and took out his guitar. He left the case open on the ground in front of him and started to play.

He was busking. If you do something, like play or sing, in a public place, and people give you money, then you're busking.

Wezi liked busking. He played some very lively tunes that everybody knew. He even danced a bit. Some people stopped to listen, and threw coins into his guitar case. Soon quite a large crowd gathered round him. His audience loved him.

The only problem was that busking is against the law. Nobody is allowed to busk in an underground station. Lots of people think that this is a silly law, but it is the law. And Wezi knew it.

That's why he didn't tell Tumeki where he was going.

Wezi busked for about an hour, and lots of people threw coins into his guitar case. Then came trouble.

All of a sudden round the corner walked a policeman. Wezi saw him coming.

The policeman didn't say one word. Wezi tried to pack up as fast as he could. He pushed the guitar into the case and tried to close it. Oh no! The guitar wouldn't lie flat because of the coins. Wezi couldn't fasten the case properly.

The policeman stopped right next to Wezi. He still didn't say anything. He just waved his hand, as if to say goodbye. But as he did so he winked at Wezi.

Wezi knew what this meant. It meant:

"You're breaking the law, but I haven't seen you. Now go away and don't busk here again."

"Thank you," Wezi whispered, and ran off as fast as he could, hugging the guitar case to his chest.

He didn't open the case again until he got home, but when he counted the money, he was lucky. He had five pounds! He was unlucky because Tumeki saw it. He had to tell her how he had earned the five pounds.

"All right," she said at the end of Wezi's story. "You win. You can take your money out of the bank and buy an electric guitar."

Now the noise well and truly reached the maximum. Wezi loved it. Tumeki put earplugs into her ears and hoped that the neighbours were deaf. Biku found her own answer. She got a flat for herself and escaped while her hearing was still OK.

Unfortunately for Tumeki the telephone seemed to ring all the time, and only for Wezi. No matter how loudly she screamed his name he couldn't hear her over his noise.

Often she had to climb the stairs and bang on his door.

"One of these days I'll get a bell for you," she complained. "I feel just like your secretary answering the phone."

Slowly the guitar took over Wezi's life. One day he said, "Mother, there's something I want to do."

"What's that?" asked Tumeki.

"Well, there's this really famous guitarist who teaches people. I want to have a lesson with him, and ask him what he thinks about me."

The lessons cost ten pounds an hour, which was expensive. But Wezi saved his pocket money and went to the famous guitarist. When he got home he looked very pleased.

"I don't need lessons," he said. "I've just got to practise as much as I can. He was really nice. He gave me two hours for my money."

Now nothing could stop Wezi. He played and played all the time. Tumeki worried more and more.

"You spend far too much time playing the guitar. What about your school work?" she said to him every day.

Somehow she didn't think he was listening.

Chapter 9

When he was sixteen Wezi was supposed to study for his GCE O-level exams. What he actually did was form a pop group with David.

The two boys spent all their free time together. Soon they could play all of the hits in the charts, but they wanted to do other things too.

They started to write their own songs, the music by Wezi and the words by David.

"Let's form a group," Wezi said one night in David's house. In fact they weren't in the house, but in the garage. They had to practise there because David's parents complained so much about the noise.

David didn't have to think before he agreed.

"We need a singer and a bass guitar too. And perhaps a drummer." David was thinking aloud. "The thing is, who?"

"Well they've got to be good musicians, but we've got to like them too. We're OK, we're into the same things. We need people who think like us if we're going to be in a group with them. We shall have to spend a lot of time together."

Wezi and David made a list of suitable people. It was quite difficult to choose names. Some of the friends they liked couldn't play. Some of the people who could play they didn't like. Some boys couldn't join the group because of their studies. Wezi found that hard to understand!

In the end they chose Dean for bass guitar, Nial for drums, and Peter to sing. Wezi and David were the two lead guitars.

Then the hard work began.

At first the group was terrible. They were different people with different ideas. Wezi found out just how important it was to think alike, to be "on the same wavelength" as his friends.

They argued about everything: when to meet, where to practise, how to play.

But slowly the quarrels stopped and the music got better.

"When are you going to perform in public?" his mother asked Wezi, laughing, one night. She didn't understand how serious he was about his group.

She should have known better though. Wezi was quiet, but he was very determined.

"Next Friday," he answered.

Tumeki was very surprised.

"Where?" she wanted to know.

"At the youth club. They have a disco every month. I know the guy who runs it, Chris Jackson. He wants us to play a few hits for them at the next disco."

"Will you get paid?"

"Mother, new groups never get paid. We'll get something out of it though."

"What? What will you get if you don't get paid?"

"Well, practice to start with. We've never played in public before. We'll have a live audience. And if the kids like us they'll tell their friends about us."

"Have you got a name? The group I mean, not you."
"The DW Boys. 'D' for David and 'W' for Wezi."

Tumeki sighed. She wasn't very happy about it. She wanted Wezi to study for his GCE O-level exams.

"I don't know," she said. "What about your exams? What about your school work? That's more important than the group."

Wezi shook his head. He couldn't make his mother understand. He had to stay at school until he was sixteen. That was the law. And if he was at school, he would do enough work to pass the exams. He had decided that long ago.

"It's all right, Mum," he said. "I'm working. I shall pass. Don't worry."

The youth club held its disco in a hall near Wezi's house. It was a big room, with a high roof and windows. It was used for meetings by groups from the nearby community – by mothers and their babies, by old people and by young

people. It didn't have much atmosphere, but it did have a stage.

Wezi and the DW Boys arrived early to set up their equipment. They had borrowed amplifiers from Peter's brother. They would be heard if nothing else, Tumeki thought to herself.

The disco started at about eight o'clock. Chris Jackson, the youth club leader, had tapes and records, and tried hard to get things moving. About fifty kids turned up, but nobody was getting any buzz out of the music.

Not for the first hour or so, that is. Then Chris wanted to take a break.

"Right, boys. Your turn now," he said to Wezi and the group, who were ready on stage. He turned to face the hall. "Now here's London's newest group, the DW Boys."

There was silence for a few seconds, and then Wezi played the first notes of "Wait for me". David, Nial and Dean joined in, and Peter found his voice.

Suddenly the disco took off as the music boomed out. At first the kids clapped to the beat. Then they got to their feet and danced and sang, and then they shouted for more.

"Wake me up before you go go", carried them further. By the time the DW Boys got to "Everybody wants to rule the world" they felt as if they were on top of the world! They finished their act in a storm of cheering and shouting.

"How did it go?" Tumeki asked when Wezi got home.

"OK," Wezi replied. Inside he didn't feel that it was just "OK". He felt wonderful, fantastic, brilliant – but he couldn't put it into words.

"Good," said his mother. "The group's a nice hobby for you."

Chapter
10

Unlike his mother, Wezi did not think that his music was a "nice hobby". It was much more than that. The two of them argued almost every day about it.

"Listen, Wezi. You're lucky to be having a good education, and a free one too," said Tumeki. "You mustn't waste this big chance. Please spend more time on your studies. Otherwise how are you going to pass your exams? It's music, music all day long with you."

"But Mother, I want to be a musician," said Wezi in a tired voice. "You don't understand, do you?"

"I do understand. It's you that doesn't understand," Tumeki argued angrily. "One day you'll want to go back to Africa. You need a good education to get a job there."

"How many times do I have to tell you, Mother? I don't want the sort of good job that you want me to have. Not in England or in Africa. I want to be a musician. For me that's a good job – the best job in the world."

"How can you talk like that, Wezi? You've got a brain, so use it. All your teachers say you can pass your O-level exams, and even go to university if only you work harder."

"Mother, I don't want to go to university. I keep telling you, I want to be a musician. That's what I enjoy. Don't you see?"

Tumeki didn't see.

"You need a safe job which pays well. How many musicians have that?" she argued.

Wezi stared at his mother. He felt so helpless.

"How can I make you understand, Mother? You know nothing about music."

"I know plenty about music," Tumeki said. She was in full flow now and nothing could stop her. "I know there are hundreds of hungry musicians out there because they don't have real jobs."

"But they're not me."

"What's so special about you? In England it'll be even worse for you."

"Why? Why worse for me?"

"How can you ask? Because you're black, of course. How are you going to be a success when all those white kids want to be musicians too? It'll be twice as difficult for you."

"If I have talent my colour will make no difference at all," Wezi said.

Tumeki stared at Wezi and shook her head.

"You don't really know what I'm talking about," she said.

"Of course I do," Wezi argued. "You're talking about racism, aren't you? That's what's worrying you now."

He looked at his mother from the corner of his eye.

"Yes. Well...?"

"Well, that's their problem – the problem of the racists, I mean. Not mine. Anyway you're wrong, Mother. There's less racism in the music world then elsewhere. As long as the fans like the music, then you're OK."

Tumeki waved her arms and stamped round the room. Why was Wezi so difficult? He had an answer for everything. But what a waste it would be if he had his own way. He was clever. Why couldn't he become a doctor or an engineer, like Uncle Kanyerere?

Funnily enough, Wezi was thinking about Uncle Kanyerere too. He remembered the words that his uncle had spoken back in Malawi.

"You have to live your own life, Wezi."

Wezi had never forgotten those words.

And he had made up his mind about being a musician. Perhaps not now, but one day it would happen. Nothing his mother said could change that.

Wezi had had enough for one night. He said goodnight, went up to his room, and played his guitar as if the quarrel with Tumeki had never happened.

Tumeki couldn't forget though. She loved Wezi. She had worked hard to give him a home and everything else that a boy should have. She only wanted to do what was best for him.

She decided to go and see Wezi's teachers. Perhaps they could make him see sense.

There was an Open Day at Wezi's school quite soon. Parents could see the teachers and talk about their children's work. Tumeki took Wezi along with her.

Wezi's class teacher sat behind her desk. She listened quietly to Tumeki.

"You see, he doesn't spend enough time on his studies," she began.

"Don't worry about him, Mrs Onyango," said Wezi's teacher. "Most boys of his age are the same. But he's doing well."

"But he could do better," Tumeki went on. "He spends all his time playing his guitar. He's just wasting his time."

"Mrs Onyango, don't worry," smiled Wezi's teacher. "He's doing well at school. And he does have a real talent for music. You must encourage him."

Tumeki couldn't believe her ears. Encourage him! When the only thing he wanted to be was a musician!

"But he wants to be a musician. Not just for a hobby, for a job."

"Let him try, Mrs Onyango. He can always change his mind later on."

"But how's he going to live while he's trying?" Mrs Onyango wanted to know. "Who's going to buy his food and clothes and, and, and . . ."

For once she was lost for words. For Wezi to be a musician was bad. For her to encourage him was even worse.

Tumeki felt very sorry for herself. Wezi's teacher just looked at her, as if to say,

"There's nothing you can do."

Chapter
| 11 |

Wezi passed his GCE O-level exams, but then the troubles with his mother got worse. O-levels were not enough for Tumeki.

She thought that a good education was the most important thing for Wezi. *Wezi* thought that his music was the most important thing in his life. There was no way the two of them could agree.

Wezi and his mother had long arguments about what he was to do. The atmosphere in the house was really terrible.

"You've got to take your GCE A-level exams," Tumeki said. "You'll never get anywhere without them."

"Mother, I don't want to take my A-level exams. I don't want to stay at school." Wezi spoke calmly, though he didn't feel it. "School won't help me. I want to be a musician."

"A musician! I wish you'd forget that silly idea." Tumeki was getting angry. "Who's going to feed you if you're a musician? Tell me that. Look how many hungry musicians there are out on the streets. How are you going to earn any money?"

"I don't care about money. I just want to make music."

In the end Wezi went back to school. He didn't want to go, but for once Tumeki got her own way. She made him study for his GCE A-level exams.

He had no idea what subjects to choose. Should he study science? Should he study maths? Should he study foreign languages? Or history? Or economics? Or what?

The only thing he really wanted to study was music, and he couldn't do that at his school.

"Choose subjects that you're good at. Or subjects that you find interesting," his mother advised.

In the end Wezi agreed to her choice of government and politics, business studies and English.

Wezi didn't enjoy his school work, so he made up for it with his music. The best thing in his life at this time was the DW Boys.

After that first disco in the youth club, people talked about them. Here was a really good group.

Their friends asked them to play at parties. This was fun, but it had its problems too. Houses were small and walls were thin, or so it seemed. Their friends thought that the DW Boys were great, but the neighbours didn't always agree. Especially in the early hours of the morning!

Equipment was difficult too, a real problem.

At first the DW Boys were happy enough with their instruments and borrowed amplifiers. They soon found out that they needed more equipment and better equipment. That was the only way to get a really good sound. A synthesiser was at the top of their list.

But for that they needed money.

"We've got to earn some money," Wezi said to David. The two of them were in David's garage. Wezi was playing around on his guitar, making up a song and recording it on tape. The tape recorder had just stopped for the tenth time that night.

"How?" David asked.

"Good question. I know a guy who might have some ideas."

"Who's that?"

"Chris Jackson. You know, the guy who runs the youth clubs. He organises gigs too. I was talking to him the other day."

"So let's talk to him again."

Wezi and David were in luck. They caught Chris Jackson in his office. He not only listened to them, he gave them their first gig. And he paid them ten pounds for the night.

Wezi told Tumeki about it afterwards.

"What's a gig?" she asked.

Wezi sighed. Didn't his mother know anything?

"A sort of concert. That's what you'd call it," he explained. "A group plays in a club or at a university, somewhere like that. The audience pays to come and listen."

Tumeki looked surprised. Did people actually pay to hear Wezi play? She couldn't believe it.

Wezi wasn't at all surprised. He knew the DW Boys were a good group. In the next four or five months they became quite well known in North London, where they lived.

The group started to get gigs in the clubs. Nothing big, but plenty of work.

People paid about two pounds for a ticket to go to a gig. Then the owners of the clubs paid the DW Boys. They were never sure how much they would earn for a gig, but sometimes it was as much as twenty-five pounds.

The money seemed a lot in some ways, but they couldn't keep it for themselves. Every penny that they earned was spent on better equipment.

Never mind. They were enjoying themselves.

Wezi's sister Biku and her boyfriend were among the group's first fans. They went to a gig in a small, dark club, full of cigarette smoke. It was a Wednesday night – only the well-known groups played at the weekend. It was too much of a risk to let a new group play on Fridays or Saturdays.

There weren't many people at the gig, but the ones who were there certainly enjoyed themselves.

"They're good, really good," Biku said.

Biku's boyfriend agreed with her.

By the end of the night everyone was getting a real buzz out of the music. They were all dancing and there were screams of:

"Wezi, Wezi. We want Wezi. We want Wezi."

Some girls even rushed to the stage to touch him. The atmosphere was brilliant.

Wezi couldn't believe that this was happening to him. And if Tumeki had known, she wouldn't have believed it either.

Chapter
| 12 |

Wezi and the group were doing really well and enjoying life. But Wezi as a GCE A-level student was a different thing altogether.

He did just enough work to get by and not to get into trouble with his teachers. But he was not interested in school or in his subjects.

At the end of 1986 Wezi got a nasty surprise. He was in his last year at school and it was time to think about university. If that was what he wanted.

"Have you made your mind up yet?" David asked him one day.

"Made my mind up? What do you mean?" Wezi had no idea what David was talking about.

"About university, of course. Where do you want to go to?"

"I don't want to go anywhere!" A terrible thought struck Wezi. "You're not going to university! You can't be."

"Of course I am," replied David. He was as surprised as Wezi. He had never thought of *not* going to university.

"But what about the group? What about the DW Boys?"

"We can get together in the holidays. We're well known, we'll get a few gigs. There's no need to break up."

"We'll never get anywhere like that. It'll be just a hobby for us. We'll never be real musicians."

This can't be happening to me, Wezi thought to himself. But it was. David was going to university. Wezi knew in his heart that this was the end of the DW Boys.

Wezi had a difficult decision to make. The rest of the group all wanted to go to university, and he was carried along with them. He decided to go too.

Tumeki, needless to say, was delighted.

"You're getting some sense in your head at last," she

smiled. "Now what course do you want to take?"

"I don't know. Something different, I think. I'm not really interested in any of my GCE A-level subjects."

"Talk about it with your teacher," Tumeki said.

Wezi did talk to his teacher. She suggested that Wezi studied psychology. Tumeki was a little surprised at this, but she didn't argue. At least psychology was better than music.

Then Wezi had to decide which university he would like to go to. It was not easy. There were so many. He had to choose a few names and hope that one of them, at least, would like him and offer him a place.

Wezi took a long time to make up his mind. In the end a university did offer him a place, but only if he got very good grades in his A-levels.

This didn't change Wezi's ideas of how much (or how little) he needed to practise his guitar.

"You *can't* expect to get good grades if you're spending all your time with your guitar," his mother said time and time again.

Needless to say, Wezi didn't listen to her.

The exam results arrived while Tumeki was at work. When she got home Wezi was waiting for her.

Looking at his face Tumeki knew at once that something was wrong.

She sat down.

"Did you get your exam results?"

Wezi had passed his A-levels, but not very well. His grades were not good enough for his university.

"You see, I told you not to spend all your time playing the guitar. I'm surprised you passed anything, the way you carried on."

"Mother, you made me take my A-level exams. I never wanted to. I wasn't interested. I only stayed at school to make you happy."

Tumeki felt very guilty. Wezi was right. She had forced him to stay at school. And it hadn't worked out very well.

"What are you going to do now?" she asked.

"I'm going to be a musician, of course. It's what I've

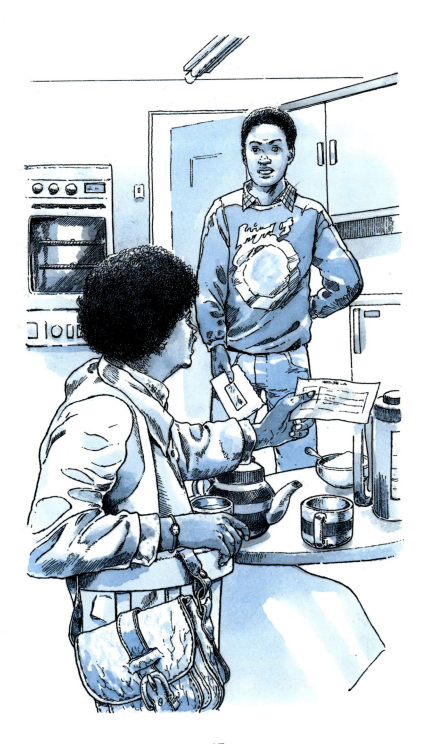

always wanted."

Tumeki didn't argue any more. She had tried to advise Wezi, but it had been the wrong thing to do. She would let Wezi be a musician. For a while anyway.

Chapter
| 13 |

Life was very difficult for Wezi. David had passed his exams and was going off to university, excited about his own plans. The DW Boys were breaking up, and nobody but Wezi cared.

Wezi didn't mind so much about not going to university. He did mind about his music and the group. What was Wezi to do next?

He hung around the clubs and places where musicians meet. Tumeki was worried about him. She had caused a lot of Wezi's problems, and she felt bad about it.

But one day Wezi arrived home with a big smile on his face.

"You look very pleased with yourself," his mother said.

"That's because I *am* pleased with myself. I've met these guys from South London and they like exactly the same sort of music that I do. And they're looking for a guitar player to start a new group."

Wezi was so excited he couldn't stop talking about his new friends.

"You don't understand what it means, Mother. Meeting people who like exactly the same music as me."

Tumeki didn't say anything about education and good jobs this time. She knew, at long last, that Wezi had to live his own life.

"Who are these new friends then?" she asked. She would encourage Wezi from now on.

"A drummer and a guitarist," he said. "And a singer too, but he's a true musician. He can play anything. Even the kalimba!"

Tumeki laughed.

"Are your friends people or musical instruments?" she asked.

Wezi understood what she was saying.

"Sorry, I just got carried away. The singer's Uzo. He's from Nigeria. The other two are brothers, Malcolm and Mel. They were born in London, like me, but their family's from Trinidad."

Wezi paused for breath. He couldn't believe how lucky he was.

"It's fantastic," he said at last. "We're really on the same wavelength, and we've only just met each other. I don't know what it is, but somehow we know how to play together."

"I know what it is," said Tumeki. "You're all black. You're all Africans, sort of. And Africans have music in their bones. I always said so."

Wazi couldn't believe this! It was true, but for Tumeki to say it!

Never mind. He was too happy to argue any more.

Tumeki soon got the chance to meet Wezi's new friends. One day they visited the house to collect an amplifier.

"Your son's very good, Mrs Onyango," said Uzo. "A real guitar wizard."

"Really?"

"All I can say is Wezi will soon be discovered. And when that happens he'll be very, very famous," said Uzo.

He said goodbye and left. Tumeki liked this polite new friend!

The new group really were on the same wavelength. A lot of groups were mainly interested in how they looked, what they wore, and that sort of thing. Wezi's new group was interested in *music*. They loved writing and performing, and they liked trying out new ideas too.

They spent all their time together, working on new songs and practising old ones. It was hard work, but it was fun.

Their music was like the other music being played in London at the time, but it was different too. Africa was in it somehow. In the beat of the drums. In the way Uzo's voice floated away. In one simple line being played twenty different ways.

It was quite difficult to find a name for the group. They wanted something easy, but something that reminded people of their music. In the end they called themselves Uzomaz, because Uzoma (Uzo for short) had started the group. It was a sort of joke, but they liked it too.

After three months they were ready to do gigs.

Three hungry months, Tumeki thought, but she didn't say anything. None of the group had a real job, there was no time for that. But they all worked for a day or so when they could. They had to. They needed money.

Uzomaz decided to make a demo tape to send to club managers to advertise or promote the group's music.

The managers could then decide if the music was suitable for their clubs.

Uzomaz recorded six of their own songs on the demo tape, just by playing and singing into a tape recorder.

"It's not brilliant, but at least the clubs will know what we do," Wezi said.

"Where shall we send it?" Uzo wondered. "We've got to get that right too. We've got to send it to clubs where they play our sort of music."

They made a list of clubs that they thought were right, and sent off the demo tape. Some of the club managers didn't bother to listen to it, but others did.

The phone started to ring.

"Can you come here next Tuesday?"

"We liked the tape and we want to hear more."

"Are you free tomorrow night?"

Most of the clubs were friendly. Some were not so good to work for.

Uzomaz had one bad time. It was at a club that none of them knew. They agreed to sell twenty-five tickets for the gig themselves. Then they would get half the money from any other tickets which were sold.

They found enough fans (if Biku and friends could be counted as fans) to buy their own twenty-five tickets, and there were plenty more people at the gig. But afterwards the manager came up to them.

"Right, that's sixty pounds you owe me," he said, frowning.
"What do you mean, sixty pounds we owe you?"
"You heard, lad. Sixty pounds. Now."
The manager told lie after lie. He was a real cheat. Uzomaz did not pay him anything, but he would not pay them either. It was a very nasty night. Later somebody told them that this manager often treated new groups badly.

Chapter
| 14 |

Gradually Uzomaz played more and more gigs, sometimes three or four nights a week.

At one performance a girl watched them very carefully. She was small and pretty, but there was something more to her than just her looks. She was so alive!

After the gig she waited for Uzomaz. They were packing their gear, of which there was now a lot, what with instruments and synthesisers and amplifiers!

The girl came up to the stage.

"Hi, guys," she smiled. "I'm Tessa."

You won't believe it, but Wezi had never really thought about girls seriously. He had looked at the fans, yes, and liked them. But he had never noticed any one girl. He had been far too busy with his music.

He was noticing this girl though.

"You guys were great. I really enjoyed this gig." Tessa certainly was not shy.

Wezi quickly decided not to be shy either.

"Uzomaz has got something special. I mean it, I'm not just being polite," Tessa went on.

"Great," said Wezi, and then couldn't think of anything else to say.

"How long have you been together?"

"About six months."

"You know, you could go a long way. What you need is a manager."

"A manager?" Wezi was beginning to feel foolish.

"Yes, a manager," Tessa laughed. "You know, somebody to book your gigs, make sure you have all your gear, that the stage is right for you, all that sort of thing. Somebody to organise things for you. And you'll soon be ready to make records. You'll need even more help then."

This girl knew what she was talking about!

"Think about it and give me a ring," Tessa said. She wrote her name on a piece of paper. "Here's my phone number. You need a manager, and I can do it for you."

Uzomaz did think about it the next day.

"That girl was right," Uzo said. "We do need some help. It takes so long to organise everything that we don't have enough time for the music."

"She knew about the music business. I liked her," Wezi said quickly.

The others laughed. "If she didn't know a guitar from a kalimba you'd like her," said Uzo. "Let's talk to her. We can't lose anything."

They were playing a gig that night. Tessa agreed to watch them again and talk to them afterwards.

"After all, I've got to know what I'm taking on," she pointed out.

The club manager let the five of them talk while his staff cleared up after the gig.

"I know about you," Tessa said in a very business-like way, "so here's what you need to know about me.

"First, I've done a course in business studies, so I know how to organise.

"Second, I've worked in a promotion company, so I know lots of people who can help you.

"Third, I'm very interested in your sort of music, and I'm sure you'll go a long way.

"Last, and not least, I'm also very determined. I don't give up easily. Give me this job and you won't be sorry."

She paused for breath.

"Now we'll be honest with you," said Uzo. "I can speak for everybody here. We do need a manager. We can't write new songs and rehearse and arrange gigs and do everything ourselves. We need somebody to organise things for us. What we can't do is pay you a lot. We're not making any money yet."

"I'll take a percentage of the profit from your music," Tessa said. "Managers usually get twenty per cent. I may be hungry for a few weeks, but I shan't starve in the end."

"You're on," said Uzo, and they all shook hands.

That was how Uzomaz got a manager. Wezi got more than that.

From the first time he saw her, he liked Tessa. He liked the clothes she wore. He liked the way she did her hair. He liked the funny way that she pulled her ear when she was thinking. He liked her eyes and her voice and everything about her.

Wezi really was very shy at first, but soon he could talk to Tessa. She had something about her that made her very easy to be with.

After one gig the others drove home in the old van that carried the equipment. Wezi went home on the underground with Tessa.

There were crowds of people everywhere, but Wezi felt that he was the only guy around.

As they came out of the underground station Tessa tripped. Without thinking Wezi reached out to catch her. Their hands met.

"Thanks," said Tessa. "I nearly fell."

Wezi's hand was burning. Tessa was still holding it.

"Tessa..."

"What?" asked Tessa. "Are you all right?"

"I'm fine. Tessa..."

"Yes?" She smiled at him.

"Tessa, will you come out with me tomorrow night?" Wezi got it out at last.

"I thought you'd never ask."

Wezi couldn't remember how he got home that night. He didn't even see Tumeki, who had gone to bed. He went straight to his room.

He picked up his guitar and the music poured out. Somehow the words in his head got written down on paper. In the morning he read the song that he had written. It was called "Tessa Today".

Chapter
15

Tessa changed Wezi's life, and she changed Uzomaz's life too.

Before she became their manager they were doing well. They were getting gigs. They were writing good songs. But there were hundreds of other groups just like them.

Wezi was very happy with his life. Tessa had lots of ideas to make it even better.

"If you want to get on you've got to do something else," she told Wezi.

They were drinking coffee in his house one night. He still lived at home with Tumeki, and funnily enough they got on much better with each other these days. At last his mother seemed to understand about his music.

"The music business isn't just about playing music," Tessa went on. "It's about being known. Being heard by the right people. Showing people what you can do. Promoting yourselves."

"And how do we do that?"

Wezi put his arm round Tessa, and she curled up next to him.

"We get a record contract, of course."

"And how do we do *that*? Send the demo tape to a record company?"

"That's one way, but it's not the best."

"Why not?"

"Well the record companies get hundreds of tapes every year from new groups. They just can't listen to all of them. So they might throw away your tape, even though you're so good."

Tessa was very sensible. She and Wezi made a good pair. His head was in the clouds. Her feet were firmly on the ground.

"I've got a plan," she said.

"Tell me tomorrow," replied Wezi. "I've got plans of my own right now."

When Tessa did tell Uzomaz her plan the group argued with her at first.

"Listen," said Tessa. "I'm your manager, aren't I? I'm getting lots of gigs for you. I'm doing all the day-to-day work so you can get on with the music. I'm organising everything. Let me try this my way."

"Explain your plan again," said Wezi. "Let's get it clear."

"Right. You need a record contract. We agree on that, don't we? Now I've looked at the record companies, and I think Vortex is the best one for you. They're honest, and they produce your sort of music. Yes?"

"Yes."

"Now we could just send your demo tape to Vortex, but I don't think that would work. They might not listen to it. Instead somebody's going to listen to you live."

Tessa paused. She had an audience now.

"I've made a friend in Vortex," she went on. "She's a secretary. She can't do much for us, but she did give me some information. The head of Vortex is called Don Duncan."

"I've heard of him," Wezi interrupted. "He's good."

"Most nights Don Duncan goes to a club after work. He goes early, about seven o'clock, and he always goes to the same club. He just goes for a quiet drink, not for the music. The groups don't come on till later."

"So how do we make him listen to us?"

"By being at the club at seven o'clock and playing," Tessa explained patiently.

"But you said the groups don't play till later."

"Next week a group *will* play at seven o'clock. And that group will be Uzomaz. You won't get paid for it, but if Don Duncan hears you it will be worth it."

Uzomaz agreed at last to follow Tessa's plan. Every moment of that week was spent working on their music.

On Monday they got to the club early. Tessa wanted to be sure that everything was right. In the past they had played on stages that were so small they could hardly move. They had played with equipment that was terrible. They didn't want that to happen again.

It was surprising, but they all felt very calm. Their songs were exciting. They had practised everything again and again. They felt good about themselves.

The only thing that they did not like was the audience. It was so early that almost nobody was around, and there was no atmosphere.

Even so, they played well. There was only one problem. Don Duncan didn't turn up.

The same thing happened on Tuesday. Good group. Good songs. But no Don Duncan.

By half past seven on Wednesday Uzomaz were giving up hope.

Then a short, middle-aged man came into the club. He didn't look at all important. But Tessa knew who he was.

"That's him," she whispered to Wezi. "Give it everything you've got."

At these words Uzomaz came to life. Their music boomed out, filling the room, demanding to be heard. They knew they were doing well. The audience, cold at first, was gradually carried away. The group worked the crowd up until they screamed and shouted, and then calmed them again with one last sweet song.

As they finished Wezi saw Tessa go over to Don Duncan.

"What did he say?"

"Nothing much. I told him I was your manager and gave him the phone number."

"What if he doesn't ring?"

"Then I'll ring him," said Tessa, smiling.

Chapter
16

Don Duncan rang Tessa two days later. He didn't actually offer Uzomaz a record contract. He did ask them to go to the Vortex recording studio to make a tape.

"You're fantastic," Wezi said to Tessa.

"So are you," she agreed.

Uzomaz went to the Vortex recording studio soon afterwards.

"I'm surprised it's so small," Wezi said as they looked at it from the outside.

"You wait till you see it properly," said Tessa.

Vortex's recording studio was small, but it was full of equipment. Wezi had always been interested in the technical side of music, ever since he took Tumeki to see the synthesisers all those years ago. He suddenly remembered that day.

Don Duncan wasn't in the studio, but a sound engineer was there. He knew everything about recording.

Uzomaz recorded six songs on to a four-track. That's a recorder with four tapes all running at the same time.

"What do you think of us?" Wezi asked the sound engineer when they had finished. He always liked to know what other people thought.

The man wasn't very helpful.

"At least you've got plenty of songs of your own," he said. "Some groups come here with just one song. What are we going to do with that? Musicians have to be able to write their own material these days. And you need ten or twelve songs for a CD disc or a tape."

"Well that's not a problem for Uzomaz. We're all real musicians. That's what got us together in the first place. We've got plenty of material."

The man still wouldn't say much.

"You'll have to wait for Don Duncan to hear this," he said. "He makes the decisions around here."

Then came a long wait. It seemed a long wait anyway, even though it was only a few weeks. Uzomaz went on playing at gigs. They went on writing new songs. They went on rehearsing. But had Don Duncan heard their tape? Why didn't he say something? Why didn't he get in touch with Tessa?

And at last he did.

Tumeki let them use her house as an office. One morning a small brown envelope came through the door.

Wezi opened the letter and read it.

"Vortex have offered us a record contract," he said at last. "They want us to record about ten songs for an LP and they'll use two of them as singles."

"Let me see," cried Tessa. "Fantastic!"

When they went to sign the contract it was all a bit disappointing.

"I thought they would have a party. Or photographs. Or even reporters from the newspapers," Wezi complained. "But all we did was go to an office and sign papers."

"And you thought you could buy a big car and move into your own flat straight away, did you?" teased Tessa.

"Well, yes. I did really."

"It's not like that. The important thing is to get a fair contract. You have to be very careful. Read everything before you sign. A lot of record companies will cheat new groups like Uzomaz. Sometimes groups even pay a company to make a record."

"Is that so bad?"

"It is if the company doesn't even try to sell the record," Tessa explained. "But you're all right. Vortex's a fair company, and I've checked the contract. Now all you have is the hard work."

Tessa was right. Making a record was hard work.

First Vortex, Uzomaz and Tessa decided exactly what to

record. They had to choose the songs very carefully, so that they were all different, but at the same time Uzomaz's own style could be heard.

It was hard to agree, and in the end Don Duncan made the decisions.

Then they had to actually record their music. They were in the studio every day for months.

"You don't just go into a studio and record a song," the studio engineer told them. "That's what happened years ago. Now it takes much longer because of all the new equipment. It's worth it though. You can do so much more with the music. Sound is fantastic these days."

They had to make a master tape, and this was really difficult. Each instrument was recorded separately on its own tape. Only when this was done were all the tapes mixed together on the master tape.

The drums were recorded first. Mel sat alone in a small studio. He wore headphones so that he could hear the engineer as well as his own drums. The engineer usually made a lot of tests before they could get the best sound.

When the engineer was pleased with the sound a red light came on. That meant that Mel could start. The engineer played a track of the song through the headphones and Mel played the drums along with it.

When Mel finished it was Wezi's turn. He put on the headphones. Then he had to play exactly the same thing, but with his guitar. And after that Uzo and Malcolm had their turns.

Wezi got rather tired of it. There was no atmosphere in the studio. He didn't like being in a small room, doing the same thing over and over again. Sometimes he made mistakes. Sometimes the equipment went wrong. It wasn't making music at all.

After days and days in the hot studio there were miles and miles of tape. Uzomaz and the engineer decided which bits to use, and put everything together on to one master tape. It was over.

The last song on the tape was "Tessa Today". Don Duncan chose it to go on the single too.

Chapter
17

You can guess the end of Wezi's story, can't you? Until his record was released he and Uzomaz still did gigs. They had to! If they didn't work they would starve. But Vortex needed them more and more. It wasn't enough just to make the record. Vortex wanted to promote it too. People wouldn't buy the record if they didn't know about it.

Uzomaz didn't always agree with Don Duncan.

"We want our music to speak for us," they explained. "We want people to know us because of that, not because we've got green hair or get into fights. We want people to know us for our music, not for silly tricks."

"I don't want silly tricks either," said Don Duncan. "I do want to promote you. That means photos. That means talking to the newspapers. It's got to be done if people are to know about you."

"Come on," Tessa said to Uzomaz. "This is Don's part of the business. He's got to promote you. He knows what he's talking about. You do your job, making music. I do my job, managing you. Now let Don do his job too. Let him promote you properly."

Uzomaz saw her point of view. They did the photos and spoke to reporters from the newspapers.

"Actually it was good fun," Wezi said afterwards.

"I don't know why you made such a fuss," said Tessa.

"It's because my music is so important to me."

Slowly the record climbed the charts. The fans who had heard Uzomaz play at gigs were the first to buy it. Word went round that it was great. When it got into the Top Forty it was played on BBC Radio 1.

After that it couldn't be stopped. "Tessa Today" became number one.

The funny thing by this time was the way Tumeki behaved. She had never been interested in Wezi's music. She had made him stay at school and sit the exams. She had nearly made him study psychology at university. She had wanted him to be a doctor or a teacher or an engineer, anything like that – but not a musician!
Then suddenly she thought his music was great! Tessa took her to her first gig. Fortunately Tumeki liked Tessa very much. She thought she was good for Wezi.
The gig was held in a very famous club. Tessa and Tumeki got there early. Wezi was standing by himself in a dark room, the stage full of drums, guitars, synthesisers, amplifiers and all the other equipment. He smiled and greeted his mother.
"Where's the concert hall?" Tumeki asked.
"This *is* the concert hall."
"Where are we going to sit?"
"You don't sit," said Wezi, smiling because his mother knew so little about the world of pop music. "You stand."
Once Uzomaz started playing the standing wasn't actually much of a problem. Tumeki's legs ached a bit, but never mind.
The club was crowded with people. They clapped and screamed and danced along with Uzomaz. The atmosphere was fantastic.
"A great performance," said a bald-headed man next to Tumeki.
"More, more," the fans screamed, waving their arms and stamping their feet.
Tumeki saw herself becoming a fan. At her age! And why not?
"These boys will go places. They're brilliant," said the bald-headed man next to her. They both clapped like mad.
Tumeki, one middle-aged fan, spoke proudly to another middle-aged fan next to her.
"He's my son. The lead guitarist, he's my son."

67

So Tumeki became a fan.

That isn't to say that she didn't still have her say – if you know what I mean.

When the group got their gold disc (for selling a hundred and fifty thousand copies) she called Wezi a pop star.

"I am *not* a pop star. I'm a musician."

"So what's the difference?" Tumeki asked. "Oh, never mind. You're a famous person."

"Mother," Wezi stared at his mother seriously. "I am *not* a famous person. What's a famous person anyway?"

"Anybody who has his pictures in the papers, anybody

who's in magazines, anybody who has a golden disc *is* a famous person. You have fans, don't you?"

Wezi lowered his voice.

"Well, yes..." he answered.

"You're in the newspapers, aren't you?"

"Well, yes..."

"You sell thousands of records, don't you?"

"Well, yes..."

"There you are then. I'm right this time. You *are* famous. I always knew you would be."

Wezi didn't say a word!